Oxford International Primary

5

W0090554

English
Workbook

Alison Barber
Emma Danihel

OXFORD

OXFORD
UNIVERSITY PRESS

Great Clarendon Street, Oxford, OX2 6DP, United Kingdom

Oxford University Press is a department of the University of Oxford. It furthers the University's objective of excellence in research, scholarship, and education by publishing worldwide. Oxford is a registered trade mark of Oxford University Press in the UK and in certain other countries

British Library Cataloguing in Publication Data
Data available

978-1-38-202011-4

10 9 8 7 6 5

Paper used in the production of this book is a natural, recyclable product made from wood grown in sustainable forests. The manufacturing process conforms to the environmental regulations of the country of origin.

Printed in China by Shanghai Offset Printing Products Ltd

Acknowledgements

The publisher and authors would like to thank the following for permission to use photographs and other copyright material:

Cover: Artwork by Dan Gartman. **Photos: p3(a):** blickwinkel/Alamy Stock Photo; **p3(b):** Winchester College/In aid of Mary Seacole Memorial Statue Appeal/Mary Evans; **p3(c):** Marco Tomasini/Shutterstock; **p16:** Rubens Abboud/Alamy Stock Photo; **p28:** Christopher Ewing/Shutterstock; **p29:** fox_workshop/Shutterstock; **p31:** Kir_Prime/Shutterstock; **p71:** Lorelyn Medina/Shutterstock.

Artwork by Dan Gartman, Mike Spoor, Kate Rochester, Chiara Pasqualotto, Chris Smedley, Francesca Marquez, Gustavo Mazali, Mark Beech, Maribel Lechuga, Oxford University Press, and Q2A Media Services Pvt. Ltd.

Benjamin Hulme-Cross: *The White Seal*, Illustrated by Maribel Lechuga, Oxford Reading Buddy, reprinted by permission of Oxford University Press.

Shel Silverstein: 'A Light in the Attic' (HarperCollins, 1981) copyright © Shel Silverstein 1974, copyright © 1981, renewed 2002 by Evil Eye Music, LLC.

Shel Silverstein: 'New World' from *Falling Up* (HarperCollins, 1996) copyright © Shel Silverstein 1974, copyright © 1996, renewed 2002 by Evil Eye Music, LLC.

Paul Shipton: *Petey* (playscript) adapted by David Calcutt, Oxford Reading Tree, Treetops Playscripts (OUP, 1998). Reproduced with permission of Oxford University Press through PLSclear.

Andy Blackford: Tchang and the Pearl Dragon from *Myths and Legends: Dragon Tales*, Oxford Reading Tree, Treetops, (OUP, 2010). Reproduced with permission of Oxford University Press through PLSclear.

Judith Nicholls: 'Mary Celeste' from *Midnight Forest* (Faber & Faber, 1987) copyright © Judith Nicholls 1987, reprinted by permission of the author.

Judith Nicholls: 'Journey' from *Dragonsfire and Other Poems* (Faber & Faber, 1990) copyright © Judith Nicholls 1990, reprinted by permission of the author.

Eleanor Farjeon: 'Bedtime' from *Blackbird Has Spoken: Selected Poems for Children* (Macmillan, 1999), reprinted by permission of David Higham Associates Ltd for the author.

Lillian Allan: 'Anancy' from *If You See Truth: Poems for Children and Young People* (Verse to Vinyl, 1990) copyright © Lillian Allen 1987, reprinted by permission of the author.

Any third party use of this material, outside of this publication, is prohibited. Interested parties should apply to the copyright holders indicated in each case.

Although we have made every effort to trace and contact all copyright holders before publication this has not been possible in all cases. If notified, the publisher will rectify any errors or omissions at the earliest opportunity.

Contents

1 A world of adventures!

My adventure

Travelling over land and sea

A Write two adjectives you could use to describe these nouns.

land _____ _____

sea _____ _____

countries _____ _____

storm _____ _____

adventure _____ _____

B Now use this information to write a paragraph about an adventure you might have. Is it at sea or on land? What is the weather like? Is there a storm? Make sure your sentences are informative and interesting.

_____

_____

_____

_____

_____

_____

_____

_____

_____

Using similes and metaphors

Read the following extract.

The storm

The fire was roaring and I was sitting in my comfortable armchair, sipping sugary tea and warming my toes. I could hear the sounds of the ferocious storm, raging all around me like a ravenous lion. My little home shook like a brittle leaf on an old tree. The piercing wind whistled down the chimney, bringing an icy chill with it. My fingers, weathered by time, trembled as I drank the sweet, warming brew. I remembered a storm exactly like this one, thirty years before, that had brought the stranger to my door. Suddenly, I heard an unexpected knock.

A Find and write down two similes from the extract.

_____

_____

_____

B Find and write down two metaphors from the extract.

_____

_____

_____

C What picture of the weather conditions has the writer created from the similes and metaphors used?

_____

_____

_____

Making multi-clause sentences

Using 'but' correctly

A Complete these sentences about yourself by filling in the gaps.

1 I like _____ , but I don't like

_____ in my free time.

2 I like eating _____ , but I don't like eating

_____ .

3 My favourite subject at school is _____ , but I don't enjoy

_____ .

4 At the weekends, I don't like _____ ,

but I really enjoy _____ .

B Choose between **and** or **but** to join each pair of clauses.

1 He reads a lot of books _____ he has never been to a library.

2 She fell over _____ hurt her leg.

3 This morning, Maria missed the bus _____ she was late
for school.

4 Johan asked his friend to come to play _____ he said he was
too busy.

5 My sister is very friendly _____ loves meeting people.

6 The boy shouted very loudly _____ no one heard him.

C Complete these sentences by adding a suitable ending.

1 I like ice cream, but _____ .

2 Tomas works very hard and _____ .

3 Tatiana loves her little sister, but _____ .

4 Tatiana loves her little sister and _____ .

Suffixes

Words ending in *–er*, *–or* and *–ar*

A Fill the gaps with *–or* or *–er*. Use a dictionary to help you.

alligat _____	tut _____	mast _____	beekeep _____
admir _____	corrid _____	operat _____	tract _____
employ _____	build _____	sail _____	cultivat _____

B Fill the gaps with *–er*, *–or* or *–ar* to make a noun. You might need to use your dictionary.

creat _____   err _____   teach _____   manag _____   doll _____

ang _____   calend _____   begg _____   sug _____   doct _____

C Use a dictionary to match the verbs with their definitions. One has been done for you.

motivate   to control or manage something

cultivate   to adjust/change oneself to different conditions

activate   to provide (someone) with a reason for doing something

operate   to raise and grow

adapt   to regard with wonder, pleasure, approval

admire   to make something go

Choose three of the words above and put them into sentences.

1 _____

2 _____

3 _____

An adventure story

The White Seal

In October, it was time for the seals to leave the beach and go their separate ways through the deep ocean in small groups. Kotick's mother taught him to perfect his hunting skills, and by the end of winter there was nothing he did not know about catching fish.

'Now you must become an adult,' said Kotick's father one day. 'You must make your own way through the ocean, alone, and come to the beach in summer by yourself.' So Kotick rubbed noses with his parents and swam away with one thing on his mind. Everywhere he went he asked about Old Sea Cow, until one morning Kotick awoke, in shallow water, and saw that a dark shadow had appeared overnight on the seabed nearby, like a mass of seaweed. But it didn't move like seaweed. Slowly it **swayed** in Kotick's direction, until he saw that it had stumpy flippers, and the most wrinkled, whiskery face imaginable.

'Sea Cow!' Kotick began. 'I need your help. Where in the world is there a beach that seals can find in summer, but human rubbish cannot?' Old Sea Cow said nothing, just turned and drifted away across the seabed, beckoning with a flipper. So Kotick followed Old Sea Cow across the ocean, swimming slowly and steadily, until she suddenly sped up, heading for the coast and a sheer cliff that **sliced** down straight into the sea.

Down sank Old Sea Cow, and Kotick with her. She led the young seal to a hole in the cliff like a tunnel. The young seal felt a sharp prickle of fear as all light was **snuffed out** by the rock surrounding him. By the time they resurfaced on the other side of the cliff, Kotick's lungs were **bursting**, and he broke the surface of the water **gasping** for air. His gasps turned to gleeful laughter soon enough when he saw the smooth rocks, the wide beach, the clean sand and the thick shoals of fish **glittering** beneath.

Comprehension

A **1** Who taught Kotick hunting skills?

2 Who was Kotick looking for when he left his parents?

3 What type of place was Kotick hoping to find?

4 Why was Kotick happy at the end?

B **Answer the questions below using some of your own words.**

1 What type of animal is Kotick?

2 Was Kotick's mother a good teacher? Use evidence from the text to explain your answer.

3 What was the problem with most of the beaches in the world?

4 Why was Kotick scared in the hole in the cliff?

C **The writer has used some powerful verbs in the story. Write some synonyms that could replace the ones below.**

Verb from the story	swayed	sliced	snuffed
Your synonym			

Verb from the story	bursting	gasping	glittering
Your synonym			

Adverbs and suffixes

Adverbs

A Change these adjectives into adverbs by adding –*ly*. Remember, if the word ends in **y**, you need to change the **y** to an **i**.

angry _____ cheerful _____ steady _____ anxious _____

B Use the adverbs below to complete the sentences.

| tunefully | soundly | neatly |
| smartly | greedily | heavily |

1 The baby sleeps _____.

2 My dad dresses _____.

3 He writes _____.

4 The rain is falling _____.

5 She whistles _____.

6 He ate _____.

Suffixes

C Choose a word from the list below, adding the *–ful* or *–al* suffix to turn it into an adjective. Some sentences have more than one possibility, but try to use each adjective just once.

| inspiration | delight | colour | power | sensation |

1 There was a _____ story about the Prime Minister in the newspaper today.

2 The professor gave an _____ lecture to her students.

3 When he sings he has a _____ voice.

4 The President was a _____ man.

5 The butterfly's wings were very _____.

Check my learning

Unit 1 A world of adventures!

Name _____

Date _____

☺ I understand and I can do this well.

😐 I understand, but I am not confident.

☹ I don't understand and this is difficult.

Learning objective	☺	😐	☹
Reading skills			
I can identify similes and metaphors.			
Writing skills			
I can use adjectives to create interesting descriptions.			
Language skills			
I understand and can use adverbs.			
I can combine single-clause sentences to make multi-clause sentences using the conjunctions 'and' and 'but'.			
I can use –er, –or and –ar noun endings.			

I would like more help with _____

_____

_____

② Travels far and wide

Commas and conjunctions

Where does the comma go?

A Put the missing commas into the following sentences. Sometimes more than one comma is missing.

1 As it is your birthday I have decided to take you out.

2 If I had a horse I would call it Silver.

3 Yesterday it was pouring with rain but today it is nice and sunny.

4 I went to see the new film at our local cinema but I didn't enjoy it.

5 As it is sunny today we are going to the beach but not for very long as I have work to do.

Which conjunction?

B Choose the best conjunctions from the two in brackets to complete the following sentences.

Example: We ate lunch early **because** we were going out. (so/because)

1 He was tired _____ he went to bed early. (so/because)

2 I wasn't surprised _____ he wanted to be a doctor. (that/so)

3 I will need to buy more wood _____ winter will be here soon. (if/because)

4 We will stay at home _____ it rains tomorrow. (if/because)

5 He stood on the box _____ he wanted to see over the fence. (so/because)

Modal verbs

A Complete the sentences below by adding a modal verb from the list. Only use each modal verb once.

| couldn't | shouldn't | must | can |

1 I wanted to play with my sister, but she said I _____ join in.

2 "We _____ get out of here quickly," Massoud urged.

3 "Mum says we _____ go swimming this afternoon," he announced happily.

4 "I _____ have come with you, I have homework to do."

B Write suitable modal verbs in the spaces.

George knew he _____ have left home earlier to catch the aeroplane, but he _____ find his passport.

"I _____ have left it until this morning to look," he thought.
"It _____ be on my desk though." There it was.
"I _____ believe it's there after all," he cried as he ran out of the door to the waiting taxi.

"I _____ run through the airport, to the check-in desk," he said to himself as the taxi arrived at the terminal.

C Write three sentences of your own that include modal verbs.

1 _____

_____

2 _____

_____

3 _____

_____

Fantastic facts about the future

Reading for understanding

A Read this extract and then answer the questions on page 15.

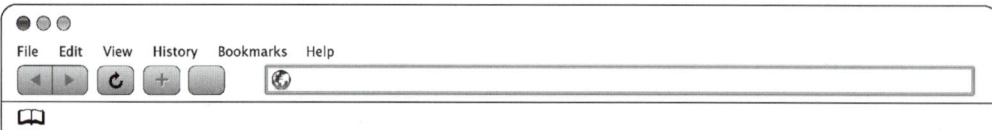

With the recent improvements in technology, humanoid robots are likely to play a bigger and bigger <u>role</u> in the lives of humans. In the future, they might take the place of receptionists, care workers, cleaners, or even childcare workers.

Research has shown that children are not <u>distressed</u> by contact with humanoid robots. In fact, children often <u>sympathise with</u> the robots and feel they have some things in common.

In one experiment, children aged four to five were put in a room with a humanoid robot. The robot was secretly being controlled by scientists using a remote control. When the children were asked about this later, it turned out that they believed the robot had shown feelings and <u>empathy</u> towards them, and that it was capable of being their friend. The children also felt the robot deserved <u>fair</u> treatment.

1 What three jobs does the article suggest robots might be doing in the future?

_____   _____   _____

2 What kind of relationship did the young children believe they had with the robot?

_____

_____

3 Did the young children like the robot? How do you know?

_____

_____

B **1** Why did the scientists operate the robot by remote control in another room?

_____

_____

2 Why would this experiment not work so well with older children or adults?

_____

_____

3 Do you think it would have made a difference to the experiments if the robot had not been made to look like a human? Explain your answer.

_____

_____

C **Replace the underlined words in the text with one of the words or phrases below. Keep the same meaning as the original word.**

feel for _____   part _____

troubled _____   just _____

warmth _____

Paragraphs in non-fiction text

Read this report about a festival in Canada.

The Carnival d'Hiver is the largest and most exciting winter festival in the world. It is held every year in Quebec City in Canada and runs from the end of January until the middle of February. It attracts almost 100,000 **revellers** from all around the world. There are so many thrilling activities for people of all ages, including snow-rafting, dogsled races, skating, sleighing and ice-sculpture contests. Children can even enjoy sliding down from the top of the ice palace! The last night of the Carnival is the most **spectacular**, as marching bands, clowns, dancers and street performers **parade** through the streets of Quebec in brightly coloured costumes, entertaining the delighted crowds lining the pavements.

A Give the report a suitable title and organise the text into three paragraphs. Make a line like this / in the report where each new paragraph should begin.

Give each of the paragraphs a subheading.

Report title: _____

Paragraph title 1: _____

Paragraph title 2: _____

Paragraph title 3: _____

B Write a short report, with three paragraphs, about a festival or celebration in your country. Include information about the time of year, how long it lasts, who goes and what you can do there.

1 _____

_____

_____

_____

2 _____

_____

_____

_____

3 _____

_____

_____

_____

C Look at the three paragraphs you have written above. Give examples, from what you have written, of the following features of a report:

• written in the present tense _____

• use of a formal style _____

• third person used _____

• subject-specific vocabulary included _____

• factual description included _____

• subheadings included _____

Building vocabulary

Foreign phrases

Some words and phrases that we use in English come from other languages.

 A Match the words and phrases below to their meanings. You may need a dictionary to help you. The first one has been done for you.

Words	Meanings
bon voyage	a drink made with hot water and dried leaves
karaoke	an extra performance after the main show when the audience has clapped
vice versa	a party activity where people sing along to recorded songs
déjà vu	a large house, often with its own garden
villa	have a good journey
tea	a loose top and trousers that you wear in bed
pyjamas	a feeling that you've seen something before
encore	the other way round

B Choose four of the above words or phrases and use them in four sentences of your own.

1 _____

2 _____

3 _____

4 _____

C Choose two of the above words or phrases and find out which language they originally come from. You may need to use a detailed dictionary or the internet. An example has been done for you.

1 The phrase 'bon voyage' is French.

2 _____

3 _____

Check my learning

Unit 2 Travels far and wide

Name _____

Date _____

☺ I understand and I can do this well.

😐 I understand, but I am not confident.

☹ I don't understand and this is difficult.

Learning objective	☺	😐	☹
Reading skills			
I can use words and phrases from a story to answer comprehension questions.			
I can read and understand the structure of a non-fiction text.			
Writing skills			
I can use topic related vocabulary.			
I can write a report using the correct features.			
Language skills			
I can use commas and conjunctions in multi-clause sentences.			
I can use modal verbs to show different levels of possibility.			

I would like more help with _____

_____

3 Closer to home

Poetry

Shel Silverstein was an American cartoonist. He was also a poet,
a songwriter, a musician and a writer.

Light in the attic

There's a light on in the attic.
Though the house is dark and shuttered,
I can see a flickerin' flutter,
And I know what it's about.
5 There's a light on in the attic.
I can see it from the outside,
And I know you're on the inside... lookin' out.

Shel Silverstein

New world

Upside-down trees swingin' free,
Busses float and buildings dangle:
Now and then it's nice to see
The world - from a different angle.

Shel Silverstein

Comprehension

A **1** What kind of atmosphere does 'Light in the attic' have? Tick one of the
following.

a Terrifying ☐   **b** Funny ☐   **c** Spooky ☐

Write one line from the poem to support your answer.

_____

2 What kind of atmosphere does 'New world' have? Tick one of the following.

a Terrifying ☐   **b** Funny ☐   **c** Spooky ☐

Write one line from the poem to support your answer.

_____

3 Write what you think is/are the most important line/lines in each of
the poems.

_____

_____

B **1** Where is the narrator (the person talking) in the first poem?

_____

2 In the poem 'New world', what does the writer mean when he writes
'Now and then it's nice to see the world - from a different angle'?

_____

3 Alliteration is when two words close together start with the same sound
(e.g. grumpy growl). Find two words with alliteration in the first poem.

_____

C **1** Three things are odd in the second poem. What are they?

_____

_____

_____

2 Which line rhymes with line 1 in the second poem? _____

Which line rhymes with line 2? _____

3 Write your own four-line poem that includes rhyme and alliteration.
Illustrate your poem when you have finished writing it.

_____

_____

_____

_____

Writing poetry

List poem

It's often easier to write a list poem if you use someone else's beginning and ending.

A Make a list of things you would like to buy if you went shopping.

_____

_____

_____

B Fill in the middle of the poem with what you would buy from the shops. Try to include some words that rhyme.

I went to the shops to buy bread

I completely forgot and bought these instead!

_____

_____

_____

_____

_____

_____

I don't think I'll shop again for a while!

Writing poetry

Kennings

A **kenning** is another type of list poem that describes something in clues without saying what it is. Each line has two words, usually a noun and an adjective. A kenning doesn't have to rhyme.

1 Read this kenning. It gives pairs of words that describe the subject on the last line.

2 Now write your own kenning about someone you know. Start by thinking about what they do, look like or sound like. Then sum up these ideas into two words for each line.

Bubble-blower

Ball-thrower

Drool-dribbler

Paper-ripper

Crayon-eater

Dreadful-sleeper

Toothless-wonder

Kiss-sender

Fussy-taster

Time-waster

Hair-tugger

Mummy-hugger

Baby brother!

Petey the robot

Read the extract below which continues the story of Petey. The Correction Squad has just arrived. Sam has come up with a plan to escape with Petey, using jet-packs.

SOPHIE	That's the front door!
	(The house computer speaks, in a flat voice.)
COMPUTER	Good afternoon. There is a robot from the Correction Squad at the front door. Shall I let it in?
PETEY	It's them!
SAM	Don't worry, Petey. I won't let them take you. We'll leave by the back door. Come on. We've got to go now…
SOPHIE	Ready? …Okay. Switch on your jet-packs – and away we go!
SAM	…Look! The Correction Squad Van. It's following us!
PETEY	Oh, no! What are we going to do?
SOPHIE	Make for the city centre! We might be able to lose them there! Follow me!
	(They zoom away.)
SOPHIE	Bank left! Through those tower blocks! Right! Left again!
SAM	There's the city ahead, Petey! We're getting near. I think everything's going to be okay!
	(Suddenly the voice of a robot traffic controller calls out.)
CONTROLLER	Halt! Stop there!
SAM	Oh, no! It's traffic control!
SOPHIE	No good! We can't stop! Come on!
	(They whizz past the controller…)
SOPHIE	Sorry! We can't stop! It's an emergency!
SAM	Sophie! We're getting away. We're losing them!
PETEY	Does that mean we're going to make it?
SAM	Yes, Petey. I think it does…
SOPHIE	Oh, no!

From the playscript *Petey* by Paul Shipton, adapted by David Calcutt

Comprehension

A **1** How did Sophie, Sam and Petey get away from the house?

_____

2 Where did they decide to go?

_____

3 What method of transport did the children and Petey use? What did the Correction Squad use?

_____

4 What reason did Sophie give the traffic controller for not stopping?

_____

B **1** The house computer spoke in a flat voice. What do you think 'a flat voice' means?

_____

2 Who took charge and told the others what to do? How do you know?

_____

3 Why do you think Sophie said they could lose the Correction Squad van in the city?

_____

4 How do you think Sophie, Sam and Petey felt when they were trying to escape from the Correction Squad?

_____

_____

C **What do you think made Sophie say 'Oh, no!' in the last line?**

_____

_____

_____

Writing about characters

Write a short paragraph each about Sophie, Sam and Petey. Describe each of their characters and how they acted in all the extracts you have read. Be descriptive and use plenty of adjectives.

Sophie

_____

_____

_____

_____

_____

_____

Sam

_____

_____

_____

_____

_____

_____

Petey

_____

_____

_____

_____

_____

_____

Check my learning

Unit 3 Closer to home

Name _____

Date _____

☺ I understand and I can do this well.

😐 I understand, but I am not confident.

☹ I don't understand and this is difficult.

Learning objective	☺	😐	☹
Reading skills			
I can find details in a poem so that I can answer questions.			
I can comment on a writer's use of language.			
I can understand events in a playscript.			
Language skills			
I can write my own list poem.			
I can write about characters in a playscript.			

I would like more help with _____

_____

_____

4 Tales and legends

A traditional story

Read this extract adapted from the story of Hansel and Gretel.

Hansel and Gretel

Hansel and Gretel were awoken from where they slept, underneath the tree, by the sweet sound of birdcall. Suddenly, a beautiful bird, with feathers as white as snow, **swooped** down from the sky and landed on a branch just above their heads. It put its head on one side and looked at them for a minute, then flew to a branch further away. The children thought the bird was the loveliest thing that they had ever seen, so they followed it. Each time they almost reached the bird it flew to another branch. On and on the children went, deeper and deeper into the forest, following the little bird.

Then, after a while, they came to a clearing, where there were no trees but a little house instead. The little bird flew over and sat upon the chimney pot.

This was no ordinary house, no ordinary house at all! This house had walls made of **divine**, golden, velvety gingerbread topped with the sweetest, most delicious, creamy, white icing. This house had windows of scrumptious, clear, melted sugar with gorgeous, **delectable** red and white striped candy canes as window frames.

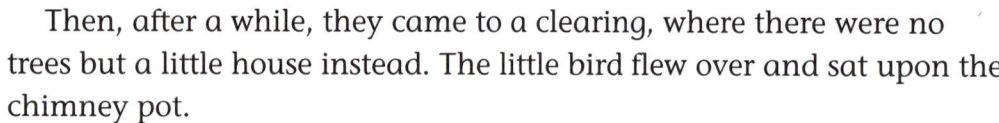

A Answer these questions using words and phrases from the extract to help you.

1 What woke up the children?

_____

2 What did the bird do when it landed on the branch above their heads?

_____

3 Were the children surprised when they saw the house? How do you know?

_____

4 What was around the clear sugar window panes of the house?

_____

Finding words in the extract

B There are eight synonyms (words with similar meanings) in the extract for the words 'nice' or 'nicest'. Find them in the extract and list them below. There are clues for some of them.

scr _____

b _____

sw _____

gor _____

dele _____

_____

_____

_____

Pronouns

Pronouns replace nouns

Personal pronouns include: *I, you, me, him, she, he, her, they, we, them, us, it.*

Possessive pronouns include: *mine, yours his, hers, its, ours, theirs.*

A The pronouns in the following sentences have been written incorrectly. Write the correct pronoun at the end of the sentence.

1 I think us must tell the truth. _____

2 Them are not behaving properly. _____

3 Me am going to race my sister to school. _____

4 I gave all the food to they. _____

5 Their house is bigger than our's. _____

6 Tchang's mother knew the pearls were her. _____

B Complete these sentences by adding a suitable pronoun in the gaps.

1 The girl thought that the coat I was wearing was _____, but our coats just look similar.

2 The leader of the group of climbers set _____ the difficult task of climbing the hill at night time.

3 You can give the biscuits to your friends if _____ want to.

4 My sister and I have short hair but _____ is shorter than _____.

5 We are going to play in the park and we'd like you to come with _____.

Tchang and the Pearl Dragon

The tale of the missing commas

 A Add the missing commas to this extract from the Tchang story.

Suddenly a great green dragon rose from the water. Even to Tchang who had never met a dragon before its tiny wings seemed too small for its body. Set in its forehead was a gorgeous pearl...

On a throne at the end of the hall sat the Great Wizard. He glared down at Tchang. "Well?" he bellowed. "What do you want boy? I will only answer THREE questions. If you ask me four I won't answer any of them."

There was his poor mother's question then the old woman's question then the old man's question and then the Pearl Dragon's question. For his own sake as well as his mother's he desperately wanted to know the answer to the first question but he also knew he couldn't let his friends down. So he answered sadly "Then I will only ask you three."

From *Tchang and the Pearl Dragon*
by Andy Blackford

 **B** Write out the rule for three of the different uses of commas within the story of Tchang above.

Rule 1 _____

Rule 2 _____

Rule 3 _____

Apostrophes

Possession and contraction

A In the following sentences, circle the apostrophes of possession and underline apostrophes showing a contraction.

1 They're going to Gomez's to ask him if he wants to play football.

2 The girls' school up the road isn't very big.

3 I wasn't looking where I was going and knocked into the man's shoulder.

4 The woman said she'd be able to fix my aunty's car by Wednesday.

5 My brother's room is always untidy.

B Add the missing apostrophes to the following sentences.

1 My childrens school isnt far from our house.

2 All the animals cages in the zoo need to be cleaned while theyre eating.

3 Ill have my dinner then start my homework.

4 Its raining so Im going for a walk later.

5 At Khans party, all the kids enjoyed his mums chocolate cake so much, they had second helpings!

C Put the following words into appropriate sentences.

1 bear's _____

_____

2 bees' _____

_____

3 girl's _____

_____

Prepositions

A Fill in the gaps with a suitable preposition from the list below. You can use each preposition once only, so cross them out as you use them.

| up above for about on along at through inside against |
| in down on across out After into to from off |

Leila was walking _____ her road, _____ her way home, thinking _____ the lovely dinner waiting _____ home _____ her, when suddenly she heard a meowing _____ her head. She looked _____ and saw her neighbour's kitten stuck _____ the tree. She tried to call it _____ but it was too afraid. Leila then went _____ the road and knocked _____ her neighbour's door. _____ Leila explained the problem _____ her neighbour, the neighbour came _____ of his house and went _____ his garden _____ a side gate. He took a ladder from _____ his shed and put the ladder _____ the tree. Moments later, the neighbour took the little kitten carefully _____ the tree, and carrying it gently, came _____ the ladder.

B Write suitable sentences which you can end with the following prepositional phrases.

1 onto the wall

_____

2 through the round window

_____

3 into the swimming pool

_____

4 up the stairs

_____

5 out of the school gates

_____

Writing a traditional tale

Getting the opening right

When you are writing a traditional tale or legend, you want to set the scene at the beginning and make your opening sentence exciting so that the reader wants to read on.

Example: Long, long ago there was a lazy hare who was always boasting, to anyone that would listen, that he was the fastest of all creatures.

A Write two more opening sentences for a traditional tale or legend. You can invent your own story or tell a tale that you know.

_____

_____

_____

_____

Making a plan to write a traditional tale or legend

You can follow your opening sentence with the following structure:

Problem/action *Example:* A tortoise challenges the hare to a race.

Resolution *Example:* The hare is so far in front he decides to have a rest and falls asleep. So the tortoise, who is running at a slow, even pace, wins the race.

Ending/moral *Example:* Slow and steady is best and don't show off.

B Write your own plan, like the one above, for a traditional tale or legend.

_____

_____

_____

_____

_____

Check my learning

Unit 4 Tales and legends

Name _____

Date _____

☺ I understand and I can do this well.

😐 I understand, but I am not confident.

☹ I don't understand and this is difficult.

Learning objective	☺	😐	☹
Reading skills			
I can explore the text features of traditional tales and legends.			
Writing skills			
I can plan my own legend or fable using typical features of the genre.			
Language skills			
I can use pronouns, making clear to what or whom they refer.			
I can use commas to separate clauses within sentences and clarify meaning in multi-clause sentences.			
I can use apostrophes for both possession and contractions.			

I would like more help with _____

_____

_____

(5) Introduce yourself

Interviews

Tennis interview

A Read this interview with the tennis player Danek Hlavacek, about the Wimbledon tennis tournament. Then answer the questions below. JB is the person interviewing Danek.

JB

> You were obviously one of the **favourites** to win, so why have you pulled out of Wimbledon this year?

DH

> Unfortunately, it's all down to my back injury. I was suffering from really bad back pain in the French Open and I just haven't fully recovered enough yet. I'm really **devastated** because I love the atmosphere at Wimbledon – it's the tournament I enjoy playing at the most.

JB

> So who is your favourite to win Wimbledon this year?

DH

> Well, it is really difficult to say. Nadal and Federer are both great players, of course, but neither has been on good form for the last few months. Ferrer has had a really good year. He's all about speed, but he prefers clay courts to the soft grass courts of Wimbledon. So perhaps this will finally be Murray's year. He's certainly been playing really well recently and he's so eager to succeed at Wimbledon.

1 Why did Hlavacek pull out of Wimbledon? _____

_____

2 Why was Hlavecek unhappy about having to pull out of Wimbledon?

_____

_____

3 Who did Hlavacek think could win Wimbledon? _____

B **1** According to Hlavacek, why is Ferrer not so likely to win Wimbledon?

_____

_____

_____

2 What does Hlavacek say in the interview that suggests Murray has a good chance of winning Wimbledon?

_____

_____

_____

Direct or reported speech

C **1** Decide which of the sentences below are direct speech and which are reported speech. Ring the correct answer.

a "Why have you pulled out of Wimbledon?" she asked. (Direct/Reported)

b "It's sadly all down to my back," he replied. (Direct/Reported)

c He said that it was a problem he had been suffering from at the French Open. (Direct/Reported)

d He told JB that it was a shame because he enjoyed playing at Wimbledon the most. (Direct/Reported)

2 Change JB'S second question in the interview to reported speech.

_____

_____

_____

Forming plurals

Following spelling patterns

A   Add –*s* or –*es* to the following nouns to make them plural.

lunch ____   box ____   cat ____   dish ____   door ____

tomato ____   day ____   watch ____   table ____   wish ____

radio ____   tree ____   glass ____   pear ____   book ____

piano ____   pea ____

B   Make these singular nouns into plurals. Remember the rules. In some words, you will need to change at least one letter before adding **s**.

donkey _____   fly _____   party _____   story _____   berry _____

tray _____   toy _____   baby _____   pony _____   jelly _____

lady _____   key _____   curry _____   day _____

C   Some plural nouns do not follow clear rules. Write the plurals for the nouns below.

child   _____   foot   _____

tooth   _____   oasis   _____

sheep   _____   man   _____

woman   _____   fish   _____

mouse   _____   person   _____

Special vocabulary

Using commas

 1 Read this information text from a children's encyclopaedia. You will notice that there are no commas. Insert the commas that have been missed out in the text. Remember that commas are used in lists, and sometimes to separate clauses in multi-clause sentences.

> Before you begin to sail it is necessary to understand some of the words used in sailing such as jibe course tack port and starboard. Then you need to borrow or buy a boat or you can hire one. Next you have to put the sails on or 'rig' the boat before sailing. When setting off it is also necessary to know where the wind is coming from. The boat travels at an angle to the wind and eventually if you want to change direction you will have to learn to tack and jibe. This involves moving both your weight and the sail but with practice this will become easy. The more practice you get the more skilful you will become.

2 Draw a line to match the words below to their correct meaning. Try to work out the correct answer but use the internet or another source if you need to.

jibe	the left-hand side of the boat
course	turning the boat into the wind
tack	the right-hand side of the boat
port	the direction taken by a boat
starboard	change course in a boat by moving the sail

B The underlined words in the information text on page 39 are special vocabulary to do with sailing.

What is your favourite sport? Make a list of special vocabulary which links to that sport. Use a dictionary or an encyclopedia to help you.

Sport _____

_____ _____ _____

_____ _____ _____

C Use your list of special vocabulary to write your own information text. You might want to include the following information:

1 How to play the sport _____

_____

_____

_____

2 Where the sport originally came from _____

3 Where it is most popular now _____

4 Important tournaments or competitions _____

_____

_____

5 The best players/competitors of the sport

_____

_____

_____

_____

Writing genres

Which genre?

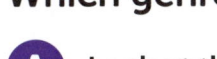 **Look at these opening sentences (1 to 9) and choose the genre of text you think that they belong to.**

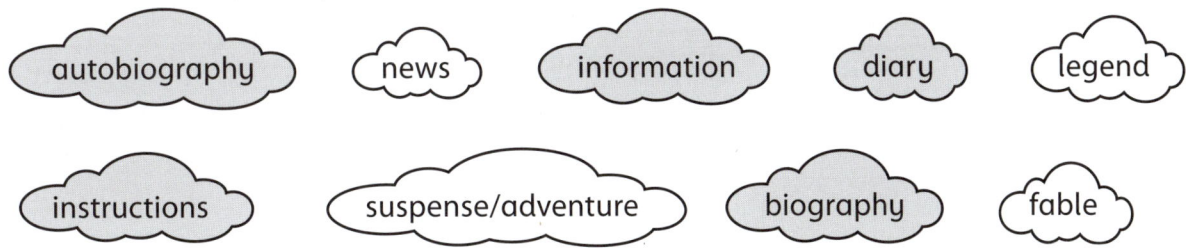

autobiography · news · information · diary · legend

instructions · suspense/adventure · biography · fable

1 Once upon a time, there was a hare who was always showing off about how fast he could run.

_____

2 Long, long ago, in China, there was a boy called Houyi.

_____

3 Dear diary,
We got up late and had Mum's special eggy bread – I love Saturday mornings!

_____

4 John Taylor was born on 27 May 1947, in a small village called Sawston.

_____

5 First take four eggs and crack them into a large mixing dish.

_____

6 As I edged nervously closer and closer to the door, the pitiful, moaning sound behind it became stronger and chilled my heart to ice.

_____

7 My earliest recollection was the day of my fourth birthday.

_____

8 The President is to announce new measures to combat litter on streets.

_____

9 The Cheetah is a member of the cat family and is found in Asia, Africa and Indonesia.

_____

Keeping a diary

Recording what happens

A Sailor Laura Dekker kept a diary of her solo journey. List three features of diary writing.

1 _____

2 _____

3 _____

B Write a short diary over the next seven days recording some of the things that you do or that happen to you each day.

DAY 1	
DAY 2	
DAY 3	
DAY 4	
DAY 5	
DAY 6	
DAY 7	

Check my learning

Unit 5 Introduce yourself

Name _____

Date _____

☺ I understand and I can do this well.

😐 I understand, but I am not confident.

☹ I don't understand and this is difficult.

Learning objective	☺	😐	☹
Reading skills			
I can find information in a non-fiction text.			
I can explain features of different writing genres.			
Writing skills			
I can write a diary.			
I can understand spelling patterns to make plural nouns.			
Language skills			
I understand direct and reported speech.			
I can use special topic related vocabulary.			
I can use commas correctly.			

I would like more help with _____

_____

(6) Tell me a poem

Personification

Poets like to make objects in their poems sound like they are people. *Example:* 'We walked along the sun-kissed sand'. Does this mean that the sun actually kissed the beach? Of course not, because the sun doesn't have lips. However, people do have lips, so this is an example of **personification**.

A Complete the sentences with a suitable word from the list provided. These verbs are normally associated with human or animal actions. Not all words are used.

> ate   winked   skipped   flew   called
> danced   played   whispered   groaned

1 The tree _____ as it bent over in the wind.

2 The leaves _____ around the playground.

3 The book I was reading was so good that the time _____ by.

4 The tasty chocolates _____ to me to eat them.

5 The fast car _____ up the road.

B Write your own sentences using the remaining four verbs in the list. Use personification to give objects human characteristics.

1 _____

2 _____

3 _____

4 _____

C 1 Write down what these examples of personification mean.

  a Time raced by because we were having so much fun.

  _____

  b The flowers were crying out for water.

  _____

  c He said he hadn't been jumping in puddles, but his shoes told a different story.

  _____

Similes and metaphors

A Choose the best adjective to complete the following similes.

| light | slippery | old | hard | free | white |

as _____ as snow   as _____ as a rock

as _____ as a feather   as _____ as the hills

as _____ as an eel   as _____ as the wind

B Choose the most suitable noun to complete these similes.

| a fish | a bomb | cats and dogs | a log |

1 The room looked like _____ had hit it.

2 She swam like _____ .

3 The two brothers fight like _____ .

4 Last night, I slept like _____ .

C Now choose the best nouns to complete the metaphors below.

| dream | lion | maze | blanket |

1 She has the heart of a _____ .

2 Life is a _____ which everyone has to find their way around.

3 I'm so happy, my life is a _____ .

4 A _____ of snow covered our village.

Spelling and vocabulary

Spelled the same but different sound

Sometimes the same group of letters can have a different sound in different words.

A All the words below contain the letters 'ou'. Sort these words into the table according to how they sound. The first one has been done for you.

| pour | favour | mouse | neighbour | rumour |
| four | south | tour | ~~mouth~~ |

Pronounced as in:		
colour (**er**)	house (**ow**)	your (**or**)
	mouth	

B Read the three words in each list below. Underline the word that is pronounced differently to the other two.

1 author   caught   laugh

2 toes   shoes   echoes

3 earn   search   year

4 freight   weight   height

5 dear   bear   near

6 plough   tough   enough

C On a separate sheet of paper, make a list of:

1 words ending in **ough**. *Example:* though

2 words containing **ear**. *Example:* year

3 words containing **ie**. *Example:* field

Say the words out loud and put them in groups according to how the groups of letters are pronounced.

Alliteration and onomatopoeia

A Write a sentence containing alliteration about each of these nouns. The first one has been started for you.

1 The sun sits staring at the _____

_____

2 The moon _____

_____

3 The stars _____

_____

4 The sea _____

_____

B **1** Below are some words that could be used to describe the sea. Match them with their definitions. The first one has been done for you.

surf	a sudden forward movement by a natural force like the tide
spray	shine with soft, slightly wavering light
roaring	the line of foam formed by waves
surging	making a loud, deep, long sound
shimmer	liquid that is blown through the air to form tiny droplets

2 Which one of these words are onomatopoeic (suggest the sound of what is being described)? Explain your answer.

_____

_____

_____

_____

_____

Narrative poetry

The mystery of the disappearance of the ship called the *Mary Celeste* is a true story. The ship was found out at sea with no one on board. No one knows what really happened, but Judith Nicholls wrote a poem about it using real facts and some made up ideas. Here is an extract from the poem.

Mary Celeste

Only the wind sings
*in the **riggings**,*
*the hull creaks a **lullaby**;*
a sail lifts gently
5 *like a message*
pinned to a vacant sky.
The wheel turns
over bare decks,
shirts flap on a line;
10 *only the song of the lapping waves*
beats steady time…

First mate,
off-duty from
the long dawn watch, begins
15 a letter to his wife, daydreams
of home.

The Captain's wife is late;
the child did not sleep
and breakfast has passed…
20 She, too, is missing home;
sits down at last to eat,
but can't quite force
the **porridge** down.
She swallows hard,
25 slices the top from her egg.

The **second mate**
is happy.
A four hour sleep,
full stomach
and a quiet sea   30
are all he **craves**.
He has all three.

Judith Nicholls

A The first verse describes the empty ship. The second verse describes the first mate. Then the poem goes on to describe the Captain's wife and the second mate.

How are the Captain's wife, the first mate and the second mate described in the poem? Use your own words to explain the descriptions.

1 The Captain's wife

_____

_____

2 The first mate

_____

_____

3 The second mate

_____

_____

B Write another verse for the poem, in the same style as the last verse, about what the ship's cat was doing.

The ship's cat is _____

_____

_____

_____

_____

C There are many theories about what happened to the crew of the _Mary Celeste_. Decide what you think happened. Write your ideas here.

_____

_____

_____

_____

Writing a narrative poem

Telling a story

A narrative poem needs to set the scene at the beginning, just like a story, with a character. Then it needs a plot, action and an ending.

Journey
I am the acorn
that grew the oak
that gave the plank
the Vikings took
to make a boat
to sail them out
across the seas
to England.

Judith Nicholls

A **1** Describe the scene at the start of the poem.

_____

2 What is the action in the poem?

_____

3 What happened at the end?

_____

B Write your own journey poem about a drop of water.

_____

_____

_____

_____

_____

_____

Check my learning

Unit 6 Tell me a poem

Name _____

Date _____

☺ I understand and I can do this well.

☐ I understand, but I am not confident.

☹ I don't understand and this is difficult.

Learning objective	☺	☐	☹
Reading skills			
I can read and discuss descriptions in a poem.			
Writing skills			
I can write a short narrative poem.			
Language skills			
I understand and can discuss similes, metaphors and personification.			
I can identify and use alliteration and onomatopoeia.			
I understand that some letter strings can make different sounds in different words			

I would like more help with _____

_____

_____

7 It's a small world

Prepositions

Choosing the correct prepositions

A Complete the following paragraph by adding a preposition from the list below.

> with   towards   in   from   of   At   by   From   by   for   in

Muhammad enjoyed going to school _____ his local village _____ Bangladesh because he wanted to become a doctor. He wanted to get away _____ small town life _____ getting a good education, _____ excellent qualifications which were suitable _____ getting a place at university to study medicine. _____ these humble beginnings, Muhammad studied hard and advanced _____ his goal _____ qualifying to be a doctor. _____ the end of his training, what do you think he did? Yes, he returned to his home village and thanked his teachers, friends and family _____ becoming the village doctor.

B Write three sentences, each including one of these prepositions.

> against   between   beyond

1 _____

_____

2 _____

_____

3 _____

_____

Multi-clause sentences

Using a comma to separate clauses

A Rewrite the sentences below to include the information in the brackets. Remember to include all the correct punctuation.

1 Muhammad went to school in his local village. (which he enjoyed very much)

_____

_____

2 He wanted to get a good education to escape small town life. (with excellent qualifications)

_____

_____

3 Mohammad worked hard and qualified as a doctor. (as he had done at school)

_____

_____

4 Muhammed returned to his home village to be the local doctor. (from which he had previously wanted to get away)

_____

_____

B Add the missing commas to the following sentences.

1 Yesterday I went for a long quiet walk along the canal.

2 My best friend who is a year older than me is going to a different school.

3 In the end we decided to go home early.

4 By this time tomorrow I will be on a train to Paris which is where my cousin lives.

C Finish these sentences in your own words. Don't forget to add the correct punctuation.

1 Since last year _____

2 _____ instead of my best friend.

3 _____ next to the sea.

Verbs

Get the verb right

A Add **was** or **were** to complete the following sentences.

1 We _____ on our way home when we met Katarina and Maria.

2 They _____ going to the swimming pool.

3 The cinema _____ showing our favourite film.

4 The children _____ playing in the park.

5 Mum _____ cross because we _____ late home.

B Complete the sentences by putting the verbs in brackets into the correct tenses.

1 She _____ (drive) to the shops when her car

_____. (break down)

2 I _____ (run) to school this morning

because I _____ (be) late.

3 Mariam's brother _____ (be) three years older than her sister.

4 We _____ (eat) our lunch before we went to the park.

5 Dom _____ (feel) sick when

I _____ (call) him this morning,

so we are not _____ (go) out.

C Change these sentences from the present to the past tense, or the past to the present tense.

1 Anya gets up at 6 o'clock every morning and eats her breakfast before walking to school.

_____

_____

2 I was running late so I was eating very quickly.

_____

3 Complete this story extract by putting the verbs in brackets into the correct form.

Tania suddenly _____ (open) her eyes and

_____ (sit) up in her bed. There _____ (be) the

noise again. She definitely _____ (hear) something this

time. She _____ (be) sure the noise _____ (come)

from the other bedrooms. Nervously, she _____ (drag)

herself from her nice warm bed and

_____ (creep) noiselessly

to her bedroom door. She

_____ (decide) not to turn

on the lights but instead slowly and

silently she _____ (open)

the door. Then, she _____

(see) her younger brother

_____ (shuffle) towards

the kitchen to _____ (get)

a midnight snack!

Synonyms for powerful stories

A **1** Match a synonym from the list below to the correct word in the box.

> sultry   chilly   devour   nibble   furious   radiant
>
> grin   merry   dim   blubber   sneak   cranky

cold ___	creep ___	cry ___
dull ___	bright ___	irritable ___
happy ___	smile ___	bite ___
angry ___	hot ___	gobble ___

2 Write your own synonym for each of the underlined words in the following sentences.

  a The sudden noise <u>startled</u> the children. ___

  b "I don't want to go for a walk," my sister <u>moaned</u>. ___

  c The plane <u>rolled</u> down the runway. ___

  d May was very <u>agitated</u> when she heard the news. ___

  e He <u>grabbed</u> my hand to save me from slipping. ___

B **1** In the story extract about Tania, in question 3 on page 55, find two synonyms that mean 'to walk quietly'.

___

___

2 Think of one synonym for each of the words below, then write one
sentence using each synonym.

a bright _____

_____

_____

b huge _____

_____

_____

c strangely _____

_____

_____

C **Replace the underlined words in the passage with synonyms which are
more descriptive.**

"What's that?" <u>said</u> Sara. _____

"What's what?" <u>said</u> Anika. _____

"That!" <u>said</u> Sara. _____

"Oh, I don't know. It's nothing," <u>said</u> Anika. "Go back to sleep."
_____

"I definitely saw something move outside the tent," <u>said</u> Sara. _____

"What's that <u>unpleasant</u> sound?" said Sara.
_____

"I don't know," said Anika beginning to feel
<u>unhappy</u>. _____

"It's coming closer," <u>said</u> Sara. _____

"I know," said Anika feeling <u>very
unhappy</u>. _____

The girls were both <u>scared</u>. _____

"Surprise!" said Mario, Sara's little
brother, poking his head through the tent
mischievously.

Sounds similar but different meaning

They're, their or there

A Fill in the gaps with **they're**, **their** or **there**.

1 As my neighbours were on holiday, I watered _____ garden for them.

2 _____ was a huge thunderstorm in the night.

3 I looked in his bedroom, but John wasn't _____

4 We are going to Eshe and Haji's house tonight as _____ cooking us a special dinner.

5 The children looked everywhere for _____ ball but they couldn't find it anywhere.

6 My friend's family are on _____ holiday in Greece and _____ having a great time _____!

Where, wear or we're

B Fill in the gaps with **where, wear or we're**.

1 _____ did you say you were going tomorrow night?

2 We were going to the cinema, but now _____ going to the theatre instead.

3 What are you going to _____ to the theatre?

4 I want to _____ my long black dress, but I don't know _____ it is.

5 Are you happy now that you know _____ your parents are taking you on holiday?

Check my learning

Unit 7 It's a small world

Name _____

Date _____

☺ I understand and I can do this well.

😐 I understand, but I am not confident.

☹ I don't understand and this is difficult.

Learning objective	☺	😐	☹
Writing skills			
I can identify, use and spell homophones.			
I can use commas to separate clauses and to make meanings clearer in multi-clause sentences.			
I can use prepositions in my writing.			
Language skills			
I understand and can change the tense of verbs in sentences.			
I understand and can use a range of synonyms.			

I would like more help with _____

_____

_____

_____

8 That's a good point!

Creating opposites, making comparisons

Prefixes for opposites

A The prefixes *un-*, *dis-*, *in-*, *il-* and *ir-* all mean 'not' and are used to create the opposite meaning of a word. Choose the right prefix to connect to the words below to make the opposite meaning.

dis   un   in   il   ir

_____ happy	_____ trust	_____ like	_____ legal
_____ beatable	_____ even	_____ deserved	_____ content
_____ relevant	_____ equal	_____ well	_____ obey
_____ obedient	_____ logical	_____ dress	_____ popular
_____ zip	_____ please	_____ likely	_____ pleasant

Forming the comparative and superlative

adjective	comparative	superlative
big	bigger	biggest
bright	brighter	brightest
white	whiter	whitest
angry	angrier	angriest
careful	more careful	most careful
confident	more confident	most confident

B Using the examples at the bottom of page 60, write the spelling rules for forming the following comparative and superlative forms.

1 A one-syllable adjective

Example: bright: add **-er** or **-est** to the end of the word.

2 A one-syllable adjective ending in **e**

_____

3 A one-syllable adjective ending with a single consonant with a short vowel before it

_____

4 An adjective ending with **y**

_____

5 Adjectives with three or more syllables

_____

C **1** Write five more adjectives to give an example of each of the above rules.

a _____   b _____   c _____

d _____   e _____

2 The following adjectives are irregular and do not follow the rules.
Complete the comparative and superlative forms in the spaces provided.

adjective	comparative	superlative
good		
bad		
far		
many		

Persuasive posters

Design a poster to persuade children to recycle plastic rubbish. You could include rhetorical questions, repetition and an eye-catching picture.

Idioms

Everyday sayings

 A Finish writing the sentences, replacing the words in brackets with one of the idioms below.

hang in there	the final straw	once in a blue moon
driving me up the wall	pull yourself together	it's not rocket science

1 Keep trying and (*don't give up*). _____

2 All the noise next door is (*making me so cross*). _____

3 We go out to dinner together about (*once a year*). _____

4 I think you should stop wailing and (*calm down*). _____

5 He was having a bad day but breaking his phone was (*when his patience ran out*). _____

6 You can work out what to do. (*It's simple*). _____

B Use one of the words below to complete the following idioms and then match each of the idioms with their correct definition.

Idiom	**Definition**
1 call it a _____	to leave
2 at the drop of a _hat_____	feeling sick or unwell
3 under the _____	stop working on something
4 miss the _____	through both good and bad times
5 _____ the road	instantly, without hesitation
6 through _____ and thin	be too late

Persuasive language in adverts

A perfect holiday

Advertisements are a type of persuasive writing. They appeal to your feelings by using strong descriptive words. Read this newspaper advert.

European Holiday

Nothing can possibly compare with the wonderful elegance of a fantastic holiday in Europe. Discover amazing and delightful destinations brimming with cultural and scenic splendour. Make 2022 the year that you cruise the sublime Scottish shores, relax on the tranquil, glorious shores of the Italian lakes or experience the breathtakingly spectacular mountain range of the Swiss Alps. Whatever you decide, you're certain to find your perfect European getaway so do not hesitate, do not miss out on this once-in-a-lifetime trip, book now to save disappointment later.

A Circle all the strong words used in the advertisement, then find their synonyms in a thesaurus or dictionary.

Example: sublime – synonyms: glorious, splendorous, superb

B Fill in the gaps in this advertisement with suitable strong and persuasive words.

Join us for an _____ journey to _____ (fill in the name of your country here) full of _____ highlights. This will surely be a _____ holiday. You will see _____ scenery and some of the most _____ cities of the world. Our hotels offer the most _____ accommodation at _____ prices. Truly, this will be a _____ experience for you.

C On a separate piece of paper, write your own advertisement using suitable language to persuade people to come on holiday to a place or area in your country.

Persuasive writing

Writing a persuasive letter

 A Head teacher Mrs Smith has decided to get rid of the lunch break at your school. This means that, not only will you not get any food at lunch time, you will have lessons instead. Max has written this letter to complain, but it's not correct for the task. Make notes at the side of the letter to identify what he has done wrong.

Dear Mrs Smith

Eating food is really good for you as it helps people to think better and this will mean that everyone will be able to work harder. I know that teachers want all the children at school to do well and they will be able to study for longer if they don't stop for lunch.

I am writing to you because you have banned lunch break. This will not help our education. I don't agree with your decision and I have decided that I would like to have our lunch breaks back. I demand this!!!!!

> This should be the first paragraph as it explains the reason for writing.

Secondly, it might mean that children could suffer from diseases in their later life. We need to go outside to get exercise and fresh air, and we should also have some sort of snack like an apple. It would be good if we could eat this during the lessons we will be having at lunch time.

At lunch break children can socialise and play with their friends. Children will not do better in lessons without fresh air.

Thanks a lot,

Max

B Give four examples of features of persuasive letters that Max didn't include.

Feature 1 rhetorical questions

Feature 2 _____

Feature 3 _____

Feature 4 _____

C Rewrite the letter, making it more suitable for persuading Mrs Smith to keep lunch breaks.

_____

_____

_____

_____

_____

_____

_____

_____

_____

_____

_____

_____

_____

_____

_____

_____

_____

_____

_____

_____

Check my learning

Unit 8 That's a good point!

Name _____

Date _____

😊 I understand and I can do this well.

😐 I understand, but I am not confident.

☹️ I don't understand and this is difficult.

Learning objective	😊	😐	☹️
Writing skills			
I can organise and write an advertisement using persuasive language.			
I can organise and write a letter using persuasive language.			
Language skills			
I can investigate ways of creating opposites and comparatives.			
I can identify homophones.			
I can identify and use a number of idioms.			

I would like more help with _____

_____

_____

_____

9 A great performance

Performance poetry

Read this poem and then answer the questions below.

Bedtime

Five minutes, five minutes more, please!
Let me stay five minutes more!
Can't I just finish the castle
I'm building here on the floor?
5 Can't I just finish the story
I'm reading here in my book?
Can't I just finish this bead-chain --
It almost is finished, look!
Can't I just finish this game, please?
10 When a game's once begun
It's a pity never to find out
Whether you've lost or won.
Can't I just stay five minutes?
Well, can't I just stay just four?
15 Three minutes, then? two minutes?
Can't I stay *one* minute more?

Eleanor Farjeon

A **1** What four things does the child want to stay up and do?

_____   _____

_____   _____

2 What one thing has the child nearly finished?

_____

B **1** Write three more excuses that the child could use to stay up
another five minutes, using your own ideas.

_____

_____

_____

2 Which excuse in the poem do you think is the best one and why?

_____

C Use these boxes to draw your ideas about how you would perform
the poem.

Performance poetry

Anancy

Anancy is a **trickster** of no small order
half a man and half a spider
Miss Muffet was sure glad
he hadn't sat beside her

5   He's unlike any of your friends
He's a whole lot smarter
He tricks and he outsmarts
He's a real fast talker

He's slow on his feet
10 a **zip** on his wit
When it comes to thinking quick
he's a wizard at tricks

He's never lost a game
'cause he cheats, **double-crosses** his friends
15 When he can't win fair
he's a spider again

Anancy is a trickster of no small order
half a man and half a spider
Miss Muffet was sure glad
20 he hadn't sat beside her

Lillian Allen

Comprehension

A If you were reading this poem out loud:

1 How fast would you read it?

_____

2 How loud would you read it?

_____

3 Where could you include hand gestures?

_____

4 Which words would you stress in verse 2?

_____

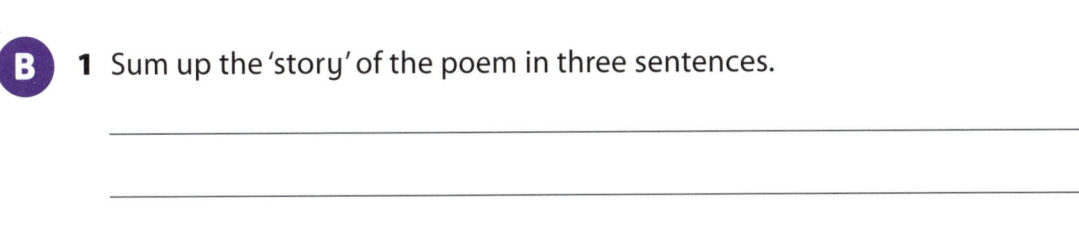

B **1** Sum up the 'story' of the poem in three sentences.

_____

_____

_____

2 Why does the poet keep the first and last verses the same?
Choose a, b or c.

a So they act like a chorus that the reader can remember easily.

b There is nothing new to say about Anancy.

c Poems should always have the same beginning and ending.

3 On a separate piece of paper, draw five big boxes. Then draw what happens in each verse in the boxes. Together, the boxes should look like a comic strip.

4 Choose one quotation from each verse and write this at the bottom of the box. It should match the drawing.

Silent letters

A Circle the silent letter or letters in the words below.

chocolate

poisonous

scissors

miniature

jewellery

B Underline the correct spelling out of the following pairs of words.

parlament/parliament

environment/enviroment

dictonary/dictionary

temprature/temperature

business/busness

C **1** Name two months of the year that have silent letters.

| January | February | March | April | May | June | July |
| August | September | October | November | December |

_____

2 Name two days of the week that have silent letters.

| Monday | Tuesday | Wednesday | Thursday |
| Friday | Saturday | Sunday |

_____

Countable and uncountable nouns

A Here is a shopping list. Decide whether each item is a countable or uncountable and write it in the correct column.

apples, meat, bananas, milk, bread, orange juice, butter, potatoes
cheese, spaghetti, coffee, sugar, eggs, tomatoes

Countable	Uncountable

B Fill the gap in these sentences with a suitable quantifier from the list below.

some   a lot of   many   much   a few   a little

1 Do we have _____ eggs?

2 How _____ sugar do we have left?

3 We only have _____ tomatoes.

4 I have _____ coffee so I don't need to buy any more yet.

5 There is _____ bit of butter but I should buy more.

C Think of two more countable food items and two more uncountable ones to add to the shopping list.

Countable	Uncountable
_____	_____
_____	_____

Performance poetry

Performance poems use rhythm and rhyme to keep the audience's attention.

 A Read the first verse of 'In My Bedroom' below. Then write the rest of the verses, remembering to keep the rhyme and a rhythm going all the way through.

In My Bedroom

In my bedroom my cuddly old bear
Is losing all his golden hair.

In my bedroom my story book

Is _____

In my bedroom my ticking clock

Is _____

In my bedroom my _____

Is _____

In my bedroom my _____

Is _____

In my bedroom my _____

Is _____

 B On a separate sheet of paper, write a poem called 'In My Classroom'. Use the same structure you used in activity A.

Check my learning

Unit 9 A great performance

Name _____

Date _____

☺ I understand and I can do this well.

😐 I understand, but I am not confident.

☹ I don't understand and this is difficult.

Learning objective	☺	😐	☹
Reading skills			
I can find information in a poem.			
I can work out how to make a poem sound interesting if I read it out loud.			
Writing skills			
I can write verses for a poem that contain rhythm and rhyme.			
Language skills			
I can identify silent letters in words in order to help me spell the words correctly.			
I can tell the difference between countable and uncountable nouns.			

I would like more help with _____

_____

Tchang and the Pearl Dragon

A boy sat on the shore of a deep, blue lake in
old China. He had been sitting there with his
fishing rod since sunrise but he hadn't caught a
single fish. Wearily, he packed away his rod and **trudged**
5 back to the little cottage where he lived.

Now it so happened that a great, green water dragon
was passing by. It was on its way home to a far-off river.
The dragon had tiny wings and in its forehead was a huge
pearl. The pearl flashed brightly in the sun – so brightly
10 that the boy was dazzled and could not even see the dragon.
He thought it was just the sun in his eyes.

The boy looked so unhappy that the dragon felt sorry for him.
He decided to follow the boy.

His mother was working in the garden, which was just a patch
15 of dried-up dirt. She came running to greet him. "Well? What
did you catch?"

He couldn't meet her eye. "Nothing, mother," he
replied miserably.

She slumped down on a log with her face in her hands.
20 "Oh, what are we going to do? This land is dried up and dead.
We don't have a thing to eat."

The boy was called Tchang. He and his mother slaved all day,
trying to scrape together enough to stay alive. But things were
getting worse and worse. There were no longer any fish in the
25 lake and very little grew in the **barren** soil.

The dragon overheard Tchang talking with his mother.
Its heart went out to them. That night, when Tchang's mother
was sleeping, the dragon gently touched her brow with the
tip of his magic wing.

30 Next morning, Tchang's mother knew just what to do. "You must go and visit the Great Wizard of the West," she told Tchang. "Ask him why we are so very, very poor when we work so very, very hard."

So Tchang kissed his mother goodbye and set out for the
35 West. He carried only a few scraps of bread wrapped up in a handkerchief.

For forty-nine days Tchang trudged across deserts and over mountains until he came to a dark forest. His bread had run out long ago and he was so tired and hungry, he could hardly walk.

40 Eventually, he reached a tiny house. In the yard, a lovely young girl was drawing water from a well. "Hello, there!" Tchang called. She smiled at him, but she did not reply.

An old lady appeared at the door of the house. "I see you've met my granddaughter, Ai-li," she called. "Please don't mind
45 that she didn't greet you. Since the day she was born, she hasn't spoken a word. It makes me very sad."

Then she looked closely at Tchang. "You look worn out! Come inside and have a bite to eat."

That evening Tchang sat by the fire. He told the pair that he
50 was on his way to ask the Great Wizard of the West a question.

"Good for you!" cried the old woman. "While you're there, could you ask him why Ai-li can't talk?"

The next day, Tchang set off once again towards the West.

Another forty-nine days passed. The food the old lady gave
55 him soon ran out. Finally, he saw a little hut in the middle of an orchard that was **scorched** brown by the sun. The land looked so dry and poor, it reminded him of home. An old man appeared

in the doorway of the hut. "Boy!" he called. "You look worn out! Come inside and rest."

60   Later, Tchang told the old man where he was going. "You're a good boy to undertake such a difficult journey," said the old man. "By the way, when you see the Wizard, would you mind asking him why my lemon tree won't bear fruit?"

Tchang agreed, of course.

65   Next morning, he rose early and set off once more for the West. After yet another forty-nine days he came to a river, fast and deep and wide. His heart sank. There was no way he could cross it.

Suddenly, a great green dragon rose from the water.

70 Even to Tchang, who had never met a dragon before, its tiny wings seemed too small for its body. Set in its forehead was a gorgeous pearl.

Tchang was about to run away, but the dragon called to him. "Don't be frightened! I'm quite harmless. Tell me why you want

75 to cross my river."

Tchang explained that he needed to ask the Great Wizard of the West some important questions.

When the Pearl Dragon heard the questions, it smiled. "You're a good lad, Tchang," it said. "Hop on my back and I'll have you across
80   in a jiffy."

On the far side of the river, Tchang thanked the dragon.

"Think nothing of it!" the dragon replied cheerfully. "That's what I'm here for. Oh, by the way. While you're there, could you please ask the Wizard why I can't fly? Every dragon in China can
85   fly – except me."

Naturally, Tchang said yes. He set off again towards the West with the four questions going around and around in his head.

Forty-nine days later, he came to the golden palace of the Great Wizard of the West. The palace was carved out of a
90   mountain. It took Tchang a whole day to climb the million steps up to the huge door. When he pulled on the bell rope, the mountain shook. Flocks of eagles rose squawking into the air from a thousand golden towers.

The great doors of the palace swung open. Tchang found
95   himself in a mighty hall. It was so high he couldn't see the ceiling for clouds. On a throne at the end of the hall sat the Great Wizard. He glared down at Tchang. "Well?" he bellowed. "What do you want, boy?"

Tchang tried to stop shaking. "I … I have four questions to ask
100   you, sir!"

"HAH!" shouted the Wizard. "Then you may as well go home right now! I will only answer THREE questions. If you ask me four, I won't answer any of them. So there!"

105 Tchang thought his legs would fold underneath him. What could he do? There was his poor mother's question, then the old woman's question, then the old man's question, and then the Pearl Dragon's question. For his own sake, as well as his mother's, he desperately wanted to know the answer to the first question – but he also knew he couldn't let his friends down. So
110 he answered sadly, "Then I will only ask you three."

When Tchang had asked his questions a thunderstorm began to rage high up in the hall. The Wizard hurled three **scrolls** down to Tchang. "Here are your answers, boy. Now go home!"

Tchang fled from the palace. He leaped down the million
115 stone steps, five at a time.

When he reached the river, the Pearl Dragon was waiting for him. "Well?" it said. "What did the Wizard say?"

Tchang opened the scroll marked 'Dragon'. "He says, if you do something really kind and generous, you'll be able to fly like
120 other dragons."

"Hmm," said the Dragon. "Well, hop aboard and I'll take you across the river."

At the other side, it reached up and **prised** the great pearl from its forehead. "This is the only precious thing
125 I possess," it said to Tchang. "I'd like you to take it, but when you get home, you must throw it into the lake."

As the dragon handed the pearl to Tchang, its wings grew and grew until
130 it rose slowly into the air. "Look!" it shouted joyfully, "I can fly!"

It was winter, now, and snow lay thick upon the land. Tchang struggled on towards the East until he
135 reached the old man's hut.

The old man was delighted to see him. "So? What did the Wizard say?"

Tchang opened the scroll marked 'Old Man'. "He says you must look beneath the lemon

140 tree."

Together they dug at the frozen earth around the tree until they came upon nine golden jars. Water poured from them, as clear as crystal. As it sank into the ground, all the trees in the

145 **orchard** burst into flower.

The old man was so grateful he gave Tchang one of the golden jars.

Tchang travelled on until he reached the little house in the forest. Ai-li was away tending

150 the sheep. The old woman said, "So why can't Ai-li speak?"

Tchang opened the scroll marked 'Old Woman'. He replied, "She will speak when she loves someone with all her heart."

Then the door opened and there stood Ai-li. "Tchang!"

155 she cried.

The old woman was overjoyed. She told Tchang, "You should marry my granddaughter. She will make you a wonderful wife."

So Tchang and Ai-li were married.

Then they set off again towards the East. Eventually, they
160 reached Tchang's home. His mother didn't see them coming –
she had cried for so long, she had gone blind.

Tchang's heart was heavy. How would he tell her that
he hadn't even asked the Wizard her question? Then he
remembered the pearl. As he took it from his pocket,
165 the light from the pearl shone into his mother's eyes and
suddenly she could see again.

Remembering what the dragon had told him, Tchang ran
to the lake. He threw the pearl into its deep blue waters. The
lake seemed to shudder and heave. Then Tchang saw that it was
170 teeming with fine, fat fish that jumped right out of the water
onto the shore.

Tchang unpacked the golden jar. The crystal clear water
poured out onto the garden and a forest of flowers sprang from
the earth.

175 Their troubles were finally over. Tchang lived with his mother
and Ai-li and their children for many long and happy years. And
every day, the Pearl Dragon would soar high overhead and smile
down upon them.

From *Dragon Tales* by Andy Blackford

Glossary

Bb

barren *adjective* not fertile enough to grow things

bursting *verb* breaking apart

Cc

craves *verb* needs something badly

Dd

delectable *adjective* delightful or delicious

devastated *verb* extremely shocked or upset

distressed *adjective* very upset or worried

divine *adjective* extremely beautiful

double-crosses *verb* betrays

Ee

empathy *noun* the ability to understand someone else's feelings

Ff

fair *adjective* right or just

favourites *noun* most liked or most popular

first mate *noun* second in command on a ship

Gg

gasping *verb* breathing in quickly

glittering *verb* shining with tiny flashes of light

Ll

lullaby *noun* a quiet song sung to children to send them to sleep

Mm

Miss Muffet *noun* a character in a nursery rhyme

Oo

orchard *noun* piece of land planted with fruit trees

Glossary

Pp

parade *verb* to move forward through a place as a celebration

porridge *noun* a breakfast of oats and hot milk or water

prised *verb* forced free

Rr

revellers *noun* people enjoying a festival

riggings *noun* ropes that support the mast of a ship

role *noun* part

Ss

scorched *verb* burned

scrolls *noun* rolls of paper

second mate *noun* third in command on a ship

sliced *verb* cut

snuffed out *verb* put out

spectacular *adjective* exciting to see

swayed *verb* moved gently from side to side

swooped *verb* suddenly dived or attacked

sympathise *verb* show understanding or sympathy

Tt

trickster *noun* someone who plays tricks on people

trudged *verb* walked slowly and heavily

Zz

zip *noun* something or someone that moves fast

Grammar and language terms

adjective a word that describes somebody or something

1. *Adjectives* are usually found in front of a noun.
   ***Examples:* Green** emeralds and **glittering** diamonds.
2. *Adjectives* can also come after a verb.
   Examples: It was **big**. They looked **hungry**.
3. Sometimes you can use two *adjectives* together.
   Example: tall and handsome
   This is called an adjectival phrase.
4. *Adjectives* can be used to describe degrees of intensity. To make a comparative adjective you usually add –*er* (or use more).
   Examples: quicker, more beautiful
5. To make a superlative you add –*est* (or use most).
   Examples: quickest, most beautiful

adverb a word that describes a verb, or how something was done. Many are formed by adding –*ly* to an *adjective*.
Example: slow/slowly
Adverbs often come next to the verb in a sentence. They can tell the reader:
How something was done: quickly, stupidly, amazingly
Example: She ate her lunch quickly.
Where something happened: there, here, everywhere
Example: After the rainstorm, there was water everywhere.
When something happened: yesterday, today, now
Example: I went to the circus yesterday.
How often something was done: occasionally, often
Example: I visit my grandmother often.

alliteration occurs when two or more nearby words start with the same sound
Example: A slow, sad, sorrowful song.

apostrophe a punctuation mark (') that is used in two ways:

1. To show where letters are missing
   Examples: don't (for 'do not'), can't (for 'cannot'), I'm (for 'I am')
2. To show possession
   Example: My dog's collar. (This explains that the collar belongs to my dog.)
   Example: The boys' cards. (This explains that the cards belong to the boys.)

clause a group of words that contains a subject and a verb. Every full sentence contains at least one main clause.
Example: I ran. (In this clause, 'I' is the subject and 'ran' is the verb.)
Multi-clause sentences contain one or more subordinate clauses. A subordinate clause does not make sense on its own and relies on the main clause.
Example: When I had finished reading it, I returned the book to the library. (In this sentence, the clause 'When I had finished reading it' is a subordinate clause, which depends on the main clause, 'I returned the book to the library' to make sense.)

comma a punctuation mark (,) used to separate parts in a sentence. When you read you must pause briefly where there is a comma. Commas can be used:

1. To separate items in a list
   Example: a sunny day, a stretch of sand, several rock pools and an ice-cream van.
2. To place a section of a sentence in parenthesis (as brackets do)
   Example: The dog, happy to be outside, was sniffing everything in sight.
3. When addressing someone by name
   Example: I understand you, Patricia.
4. After a subordinate clause that starts a sentence
   Example: Although it is cold, I am warm.
5. After many connecting conjunctions that we use to start a sentence
   Example: However, penguins can get cold…

conjunction a word used to link words or clauses within a sentence
Examples: and, but, so, until, when, as
Example: He was running when he went to the shops.

contraction when an apostrophe is used to show that letters have been removed from a word
Examples: didn't (for 'did not'), it's (for 'it is')

definition an explanation of the meaning of a word
Example: **purse** a small bag for holding money

dialogue an oral or written conversation

direct speech when speech marks are used to show that someone is speaking
Example: "Can I talk to you please?" asked Sam.

formal language standard English that we use for school work, official letters and formal settings. In formal language we avoid using contractions, slang words, lots of exclamation marks or capital letters for emphasis.

genre a type of writing
Examples: poetry, fantasy and non-fiction

homophone one of two or more words that sound the same but have different meanings. They may have the same or different spellings.
Examples: right, write, meat, meet

idiom a colourful expression that cannot be understood from the meaning of its separate words
Example: It's raining cats and dogs.
(This means that it is raining very hard.)

imperative the form of the verb used to make commands
Example: Go away!

informal language language we use in everyday settings, at home, with friends, via text messages. In writing it includes contractions, slang words and capital letters for emphasis.

metaphor a way of speaking or writing in which one thing is actually said to be something else. This way of speaking or writing is called a figure of speech.
Example: This man is a lion in battle. (This means that he is very brave.)

modal verbs used with a verb to show what is possible, or necessary or what is going to happen
Example: I **should** go for a run.

narrator the person telling a story

noun a word that names something or somebody
Examples: fox, chicken, brother, rock
Nouns can be singular (dog) or plural (dogs). A collective noun refers to a group.
Example: a **flock** of birds
A proper noun begins with a capital letter and names a person, a place or something specifically.
Examples: Mrs Brown, London

paragraph a group of sentences that a piece of writing is divided into. Each paragraph begins on a new line.

personification the technique of giving human qualities to things that are not human, such as an animal, concept or inanimate object
Example: The sun beamed happily while the kittens played hide-and-seek, and life danced by.

phrase a small group of words that forms part of a clause. Phrases do not make sense on their own.

plot what happens in a story, film or play

prefix a word or syllable placed at the beginning of a word to modify its meaning
Examples: In the word 'misunderstand', the prefix *mis–* makes the word 'understand' mean 'not understand correctly'. In the word 'unhappy', the prefix *un–* makes the word 'happy' mean 'not happy'.

preposition a word that indicates place (on, in), direction (over, beyond) or time (during, on) among others
Examples: I put the book **in** the drawer. I read my book **during** lunch.

pronoun a word that can replace a noun
Examples: I, me, mine, myself

reported speech when you report someone's words in a changed form
Example: "I am at home." (direct speech)
She said she was at home. (reported speech)

rhyme when the endings of words sound similar
Example: **bat** and **mat**, **batter** and **matter**

rhythm a regular pattern of beats in poetry

sentence a group of words that expresses a complete thought. All sentences begin with a capital letter and end with a full stop, question mark or exclamation mark. There are four types of sentences:

1   Statements – that declare something and end in a full stop (.).
    Example: The class yelled in triumph.
2   Questions – that ask something and end in a question mark (?).
    Example: Where is the dog?
3   Exclamations – that exclaim and end in an exclamation mark (!).
    Example: I'm so tired!
4   Imperatives – that command or instruct and can end either in a full stop or an exclamation mark.
    Example: Put on your coat right away!

Single-clause sentences are made up of one clause.
Example: I am hungry.
Multi-clause sentences are made up of two or more main clauses, usually joined by a conjunction.
Example: I am hungry and I am thirsty.

simile a figure of speech in which two things are compared using the linking words 'like' or 'as'
Example: In battle, he was as brave as a lion.

singular/plural *singular* refers to one thing and *plural* refers to more than one thing
Examples:
dog (singular)   dogs (plural)
sky (singular)   skies (plural)
wolf (singular)   wolves (plural)

sub-heading comes below a heading and indicates to the reader the contents of smaller units of text

subordinate clause See *clause*

suffix a word or syllable placed at the end of a word to modify its meaning
Example: In the word 'tasteless' the suffix *–less* makes the word 'tasteless' mean 'with no taste'.

superlative See *adjective*

syllable a unit of pronunciation that forms part of or the whole of a word. English words consist of one or more syllables. Each syllable always contains one speech vowel. This may have one or more speech consonants before and/or after it.
Examples: 1 syllable - house, 2 syllables - kettle, 3 syllables - butterfly

synonym a word or phrase that means exactly or nearly the same as another word or phrase in the same language
Example: Shut is a synonym of *close.*

tense a verb form that shows whether events happen in the past, present or the future
Examples:
The Pyramids are on the west bank of the River Nile. (present tense)
They were built as enormous tombs. (past tense)
They will stand for centuries to come. (future tense)
Most verbs change their spelling by adding *–ed* to form the **past tense**.
Example: walk/walked
Some have irregular spellings.
Example: catch/caught
Most verbs use 'will' to form the **future tense**.
Example: I will go to school tomorrow.

verb shows the action in a sentence and can express a process or state

1   *Verbs* are often known as 'doing', 'being', 'action' or 'happening' words.
    Example: The boys **run** down the hill.
    (In this sentence the word 'run' is the *verb*.)
2   Sometimes several words make up the *verb*.
    Example: The boys **are running**.
    (In this case *running* is the main verb and *are* is an extra verb that adds to the meaning. It is called an *auxiliary verb*.)

vowel is one of the five letters in writing **a**, **e**, **i**, **o** or **u**. In speech, a *vowel* is a sound made with the mouth open and the airway unobstructed. Each syllable in a word has one *vowel* sound.

Key words to help you at school

These words will help you with all your subjects at school.

abstract *adjective* to do with ideas and not with physical things you can see or touch

Truth, hope and danger are all abstract ideas.

approach *verb* to come near

As they approached the house, they saw a dog.

attach *verb* to fix or fasten one thing to another

Attach the photograph to the form with a paperclip.

certain *adjective* when you know something is definitely true

Are you certain that cake is for you?

comment *noun* a remark or opinion

Add a comment to your partner's story.

conclude *verb* to end something

Now conclude your story.

condition *noun* the state which a person or thing is in

This bike is in good condition.

correction *noun* putting mistakes right

I've made some corrections to your letter.

definitely *adverb* without doubt

I'll definitely be there!

discovery *noun* finding or learning about something by chance or for the first time

The discovery was exciting!

emphasis *noun* special importance given to something or extra attention drawn to something

Add an exclamation mark for emphasis.

extraordinary *adjective* unusual or very strange

It was an extraordinary sight.

interest *noun* wanting to look or listen or take part in something

The monument was a place of interest.

interview *noun* a meeting with someone to ask them questions or discuss something

Interview a friend about their hobby.

investigate *verb* find out as much as you can about something

Did you hear that noise? Let's investigate!

Key words to help you at school

involve *verb* to take part

Involve the audience by asking them questions.

memorable *adjective* easy to remember

He has a memorable name.

motivate *verb* make someone keen to achieve something

The captain of the team needs to motivate his players.

operate *verb* to make something work

Do you know how to operate the camera?

opposite *adjective* 1. facing *She lives on the opposite side of the road to me.*

2. completely different *They went in opposite directions.*

opposite *noun* completely different

'Happy' is the opposite of 'sad'.

possible *adjective* able to exist, happen

It is possible to fly to the moon.

prepare *verb* to get something ready

He was preparing lunch.

produce *verb* to make or create something

Do you think the tree will produce lots of apples?

proofread *verb* to read and mark corrections

I need to proofread my story.

resolution *noun* how a problem was solved

What is the resolution of your story?

standard *adjective* of the usual or ordinary kind

Try to use standard English, instead of non-standard English.

strategy *noun* a plan to achieve or win something

What is our strategy for the match?

suitable *adjective* satisfactory or right for a particular person, purpose or occasion

Add a suitable adjective to the sentence.

summary *noun* a short report of the main points of something said or written

Give me a summary of what happened.

theory *noun* an idea or set of ideas suggested to explain something

I have a theory about that.

viewpoint *noun* someone's opinion or perspective

Tell the story from another character's viewpoint.

1 **Choose the word to complete each sentence.**

conclude   definitely   discovery   theory   certain

a We can _____ that Amir took the biscuits.

b Amir _____ took the biscuits.

c The _____ of crumbs on Amir's bed told us he took the biscuits.

d My _____ is that Amir took the biscuits.

e I am _____ that Amir took the biscuits.

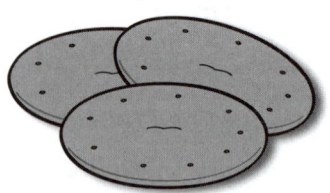

2 **Find the following words hidden in the square.**

active   interest

approach   opposite

attach   possible

announce   prepare

a	c	t	i	v	e	a	p	r	a	r	v
n	f	n	p	r	e	p	a	r	e	a	a
n	r	e	y	t	t	o	u	b	d	p	g
o	i	h	u	h	m	a	m	t	c	p	h
u	n	e	r	s	t	b	l	t	y	r	n
n	t	v	a	r	i	e	t	a	x	o	v
c	e	o	p	p	o	s	i	t	e	a	i
e	r	v	t	e	s	s	c	t	i	c	a
o	e	u	a	n	v	a	e	a	c	h	t
l	s	e	y	b	a	p	u	c	r	e	s
t	t	s	h	r	a	c	o	h	a	r	r
o	p	o	s	s	i	b	l	e	i	t	y

3 Write the words in the correct box.

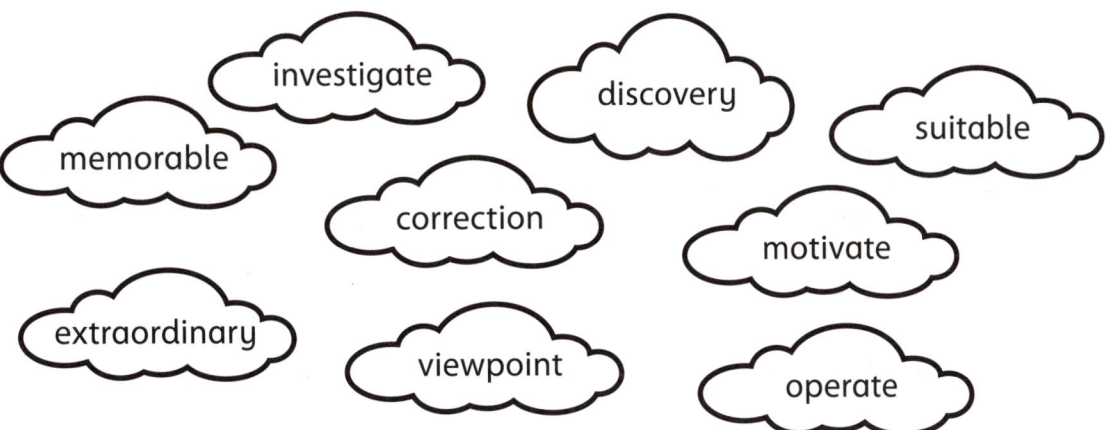

nouns	verbs	adjectives

4 Circle the word that is the odd one out in each line.

a interview   standard   discussion

b correct   proofread   operate

c definitely   summary   conclusion

d strategy   plan   emphasis

e resolution   motivate   encourage

f produce   involve   make

5 Draw a line to match each word to its synonym.

viewpoint   get ready

discovery   common

standard   amazing

operate   use

certain   find

extraordinary   talk

comment   opinion

prepare   definite

6 Circle the word that has the same meaning as the word in the box.

a   include

Jem and Al tried to involve the new boy in their game of football.

b   explore

Let's investigate that enormous cave along the coast.

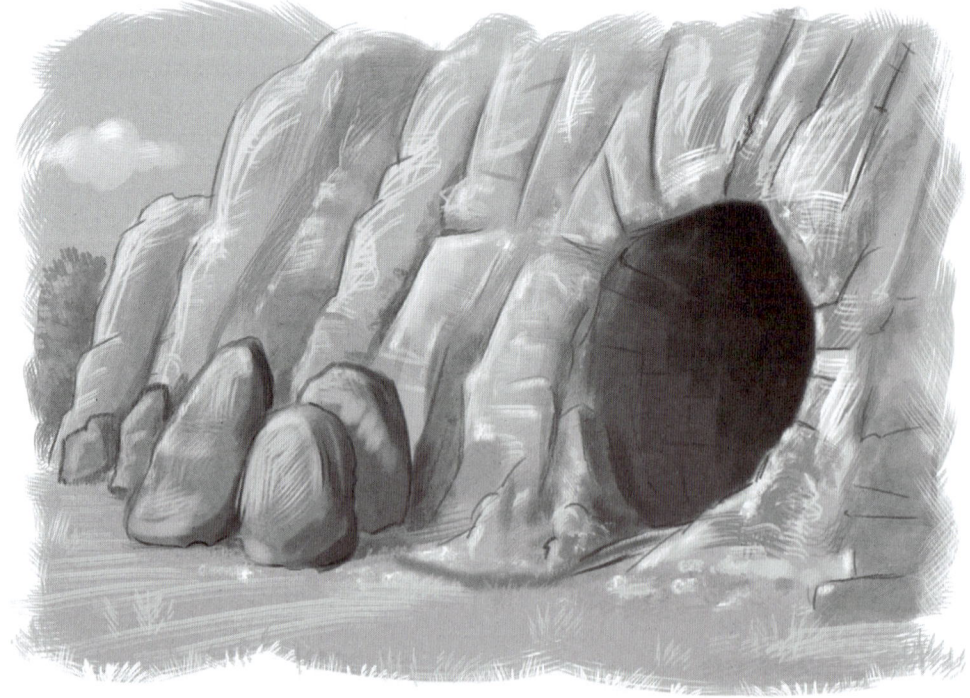

c memorable

The family's holiday to the seaside was unforgettable.

d opposite

We should have turned the other way at the junction.

e approach

Let's have a break and then try and tackle the problem in a different way.

f doable

If possible, could we go to the shops today?